The Local Church:

Her Posture, Her Purpose, Her Proclamation and Her Power

by
Ray Ciervo

Destiny Image Publishers
P.O. Box 310
Shippensburg, PA 17257-0310
"Speaking to the Purposes of God for this Generation"

ISBN 1-56043-065-6

For Worldwide Distribution
Printed in the U.S.A.

Dedication

In memory of my parents Guiseppe and Vincenza (Joe and Vinnie), for the life they gave me.

And He gave some as apostles, and some as prophets, and some as evangelists, and some as pastors and teachers, for the equipping of the saints for the work of service, to the building up of the body of Christ; until we all attain to the unity of the faith, and of the knowledge of the Son of God, to a mature man, to the measure of the stature which belongs to the fulness of Christ.

Ephesians 4:11-13

Contents

Foreword

Expressing the person of Christ to the world has long been acknowledged as the mission of the church. But how is the church to do it? What are its equipment and methods? As the body of Christ on the earth the church has a key identity to help her accomplish her mission. The Scripture clearly says, "our citizenship is in heaven", that we are aliens on the earth. It is through identifying this particular trait that enables the church to keep her mission in focus. When the church loses her identity she loses the sense of her mission because she becomes part of the world. The church's identity is heavenly, from Heaven she derives her strength and life.

When the church maintains her identity as from Heaven, alien, she is free to pursue her mission on the earth. It facilitates her to be unattached to the world's values. She can keep the kingdom of God and His purposes in focus. It is when the church loses this aspect of her identity that humanism and feminism creep in and she adapts to an earthly identity.

For successful mission the church must maintain an alien identity. Without it she is just a temporal entity, there is no hope for the eternal. With it she is undefeatable, pregnant with purpose, resolved to honor her Master and Savior in mission. With it her message is clear, simple and powerful.

This book is written as it was spoken, to the local church. Although it addresses the individual, it is meant for the local church context. When individuals join the corporate, not to lose their identity, but to make the corporate a reality, God empowers the church. The New Testament writers wrote for church minded people, not for individualistic persons seeking self-identity on their own. Among God's people we find our identity in Him; for we are His body.

Introduction

The failure of so many of our fellow Christians these days deeply troubles us all. Witnessing their tragedy, at times, our souls cry out to God, "WHY?"

I believe God has given me some answers for our times. I am convinced that many believers fail because of one or more of the following reasons:

1. They have not been able to recognize their true identity.

2. They have not known what is their God-given mission in life.

3. They are unsure of their message.

4. They have not learned the source of their sustenance.

This book brings a very simple message but one, I believe, which can change your life dramatically. You can know your identity; you can know your mission; you can know your message; and you can know the source of your sustenance. You can be sure. You have a divine purpose in life. You need not fail. You can stand in these last days—in the knowledge of God's Word—and be victorious.

If reading these pages can help YOU to discover YOUR identity, mission, message and sustenance, I shall have been richly rewarded for the effort that went into their publication.

Ray Ciervo

Part I

The Local Church:

Her Posture

Chapter One

The Melting Pot Problem

Peter, an apostle of Jesus Christ, to those who reside as aliens, scattered throughout Pontus, Galatia, Cappadocia, Asia, and Bithynia, who are chosen according to the foreknowledge of God the Father, by the sanctifying work of the Spirit, that you may obey Jesus Christ and be sprinkled with His blood: May grace and peace be yours in fullest measure. Blessed be the God and Father of our Lord Jesus Christ, who according to His great mercy has caused us to be born again to a living hope through the resurrection of Jesus Christ from the dead.

1 Peter 1:1-3

To those who reside as aliens. Some versions of the Bible translate *alien* as *stranger*. One translation uses the word *pilgrim*. The meaning is clear. We Christians are aliens in this world. We are strangers and pilgrims. We don't belong here. We don't fit into this world's system. We are just pilgrims, passing through—on our way to a totally different type of land. Recognizing the fact that we are aliens here is vital to the success of our Christian mission.

One of the greatest temptations to the believer is to settle down in this world, to grow comfortable with its atmosphere, and to lose sight of the fact that we are destined to a greater realm. We don't belong here. God has taken us from being sons and daughters of Adam and made us His own sons and daughters. He has left us here only to accomplish His mission. When we look back from eternity, we will call this "mission earth." This is not our permanent dwelling.

We must be faithful to our identity as aliens in this world, first, to remain faithful to God and, secondly, to maintain a relevant message to the world in which we live.

Although our mission is to the earth, we must never become earthly. We are heavenly creatures. We are foreigners here. The contradiction of being heavenly creatures with a message to the earth must never overwhelm us. We are not here to be overcome by earth's lure, we are here to overcome earth's lure with Heaven's glory.

We must face facts. We are foreigners here. We don't belong. We will never feel at home in this world. We must never get too comfortable here. Those of the earth will never understand us very well. We think differently. We talk differently. We act differently. Our moral values are different. We are destined for the heavenlies. That is why the world is at war with us.

Paul said to the Corinthians:

Do not be bound together with unbelievers; for what partnership have righteousness and lawlessness, or what fellowship has light with darkness?

2 Corinthians 6:14

He was not just referring to marriage. Any contractual agreement which we have with the world is uncomfortable for everyone concerned. There can be no agreement, no reconciling of positions. We are too different.

An Old Testament law forbid yoking together different kind of animals.

You shall not plow with an ox and a donkey together.
Deuteronomy 22:10

An ox and a donkey are totally different creatures. They are not built the same. They don't pull in the same way. If they are yoked together, they pull against each other and one of them will be injured eventually. In the same way, the children of this world and the children of our God cannot possibly pull together.

The most common reason that many Christians fail in their mission is simply because they fail to understand their identity as children of God, citizens of His eternal Kingdom. Just as family history and family heritage are important to us in the natural, our spiritual history and heritage are important to our continued spiritual well-being. What has happened to my own family in the American "melting pot" serves as a strong illustration of this truth.

My father's grandparents came to America from Naples, Italy; and my mother's parents immigrated from Sicily. In those early generations in America, there was a strong Italian influence in the family. Mom was the third in a family of ten children and, before she started school, she spoke nothing but Italian. I remember the strong influence of my maternal grandparents.

By the time I was growing up, however, things were changing—drastically. I understood conversational Italian, but spoke it very little. And by the time I was a grown man, I had forgotten Italian altogether. One of my sons studied Italian in high school. He never heard it at home.

Are we Italian? We have Italian names and still know how to enjoy good Italian food, but that's about the extent of it. The American "melting pot" has robbed us of the further benefits of our natural identity. For anyone who isn't familiar with the "melting pot" phenomena, let me explain it a little:

Over a period of more than a hundred years, millions of people came to America from all parts of Europe and Asia. They were welcomed here, for the most part, but they were expected to become Americans—that is they were expected to learn to speak American English; they were expected to dress in the American way; and they were expected to conduct themselves in the American way.

In time, the differences between various nationalities disappeared and all the nations were melted together. They all became simply "Americans." Many couples of diverse ethnic background married, further obscuring the original family lines. This phenomena was known as "the melting pot."

It must be said that the American culture had many good things to offer and that adapting to an "American way of life" was not always bad. But the point I want to make is that "the melting pot" robbed us of our ethnic heritage.

We have an Italian family name. My grandparents were born in Italy. I know my grandmother's maiden name and my mother's maiden name, both Italian. But that is about the limit of our being Italian. We are now Americans in every sense of the word.

Only recently have many Americans realized that, through the effects of the melting pot, we lost something very valuable. Most people would give anything to be able to speak two languages, while we willingly gave up our second language in order to be considered true Americans. We didn't value our heritage.

Some of us now regret that. Poles, Romanians, Irish, and other ethnic peoples are reaching into their past to try to regain some of the cultural richness that was lost over the generations. Some of us are now calling ourselves "Italian-Americans." The truth is that we know little more about our Italian heritage than how to eat Italian foods.

I think you see my point. The influence of the earth works to strip us of our heavenly identity. We have a great heritage. We come from a royal line. We were born from above. Our citizenship is in Heaven. We must not let that great heritage slip away from us. Some people try to maintain the Christian name, while dropping most of the Christian character. This also doesn't work. The name without the power leads only to hypocrisy.

In various parts of the world, when portions of the Christian message have been adopted but have been mixed with local religious or philosophies, a syncretism has resulted, a mixture of beliefs. The result has not been righteousness. Christianity doesn't mix with this world's religions or philosophy. Worshiping God means allowing Him to be God; and when He is God of your life, every other influence must give way. He must be Lord of all or He won't be Lord at all. Syncretism does not exist only in Africa and Asia. We are also guilty of taking what we like and leaving the rest, of taking what seems to be to our advantage and leaving what makes demands upon us.

If we intend to make Heaven our home, we must make a conscious decision not to water down our identity. We have a great history. We were born of the Spirit of God into the family of the King. He gave us the privilege of being citizens of His Kingdom. We must not deny that history in any way.

Christians who have been ashamed of their spiritual heritage and have decided to conform more to the lifestyle of those around them have fallen. These two worlds don't mix. We are either heavenly or earthly, not both.

When you deny your heavenly heritage, it becomes impossible for you to fulfill your mission here on earth. Your light is dimmed. You fade into the crowd and become a meaningless statistic.

The message of the Church has often seemed unclear, contradictory or even hypocritical—because we have lost our identity. We have become irrelevant to the world. If we are not different, we have nothing special to offer. If we are not sure why we exist, how can we expect the world to understand why we exist?

Standing up proudly for your family, taking a stand for your position as "stranger" and "pilgrim" in this world, will do more than anything else to strengthen your position and set you on a course to victory in the Christian life.

Why should we give up the great truths we have garnered in the faith and exchange them for *the weak and worthless elemental things* of this world (Galatians 4:9)? Why would we be willing to give up the accomplishments of years of struggle in the faith for some obscure recognition by our neighbors and friends? It isn't worth it, believe me. In C.S. Lewis's famous book, *The Screwtape Letters*, an older demon (Screwtape) wrote to a younger one, instructing him how to keep Christians from being successful in life. He said:

> Let them sing. Let them go to church; let them preach; and even let them pray for each other. But never let them find out who they are. The moment they discover who they are, we have lost.

The enemy of our soul is working overtime to keep us from discovering who we really are. Recognizing your Christian roots strengthens your position against every evil force. Disavowing your spiritual heritage, on the other hand, pulls the rug out from under your feet. Don't give your enemy the satisfaction.

Chapter Two

A Heavenly Perspective

Two men look through the prison bars.
One sees mud.
The other sees stars.

Author unknown

When you know that you are aliens in this world, it helps you to maintain a heavenly perspective. Nothing is more important in your Christian life than your perspective, how you look at things.

Do you look at life as one whole? Or do you look at it as a collection of individual parts? Do you look at it starting with God? Do you see it through His eyes? Or do you see it through your own eyes? Do you see it through despair? Or do you see it through hope? Are you the eternal pessimist? Or are you the eternal optimist?

It is all a matter of perspective!

The two men in this little rhyme were looking at the exact same scene, yet they saw things from a different perspective. One was looking up, and the other was looking down.

What would you see?

How do you look at life?

As Christians, we must learn to look at things through God's eyes. We must see things from the position in which He has placed us. If we look at things through the circumstances in which we happen to find ourselves, rarely will we muster enough faith to make it through the ordeals ahead. If, however, we look at things from the position in which God has placed us, we have a completely different perspective. God sees us *seated...above all rule and authority* with Christ (Ephesians 1:20-21). If we can see ourselves in that way, instead of seeing ourselves in the mess we are in, everything changes. We have a totally different perspective.

Are you earthbound? Or are you heaven-bound? If you are always thinking about your body, you are earthbound. If you concentrate on your appetites, your selfish desires, you are earthbound. Those who are heaven-bound give more attention to their spirit, to the things that God is doing in their lives, to the situations into which God has placed them and to the truths which He is working to make plain to them.

Jacob and Esau were twins. They were born of the same father and mother into the same set of circumstances. Since Esau was the firstborn, he had a natural advantage in life over his brother. Yet it was Jacob who excelled, and not Esau. Esau was earthbound. He had an earthly perspective. He sold his birthright for a single meal. He could not see beyond his present hunger to the value of his heritage as the firstborn. To him, the most important thing in the world was to eat something that smelled good. He was willing to give up his identity for something so trivial.

Jacob, on the other hand, was determined to have God's best. He was determined to be all that God had ordained for him to be. Although he faced an uphill battle and struggled for years with life's circumstances, he ultimately prevailed because his perspective was heavenward. It was not accidental that he had a vision of heaven's ladder. He had eyes to see the eternal.

Like Esau, many of us are very short-sighted. We are willing to mortgage the future for a momentary good time in life. We are willing to risk all for trivial things that make us comfortable now.

By the time Esau realized his mistake, it was too late. The reality of his loss was bitter. The Scriptures declare:

> *See to it that no one comes short of the grace of God; that no root of bitterness springing up causes trouble, and by it many be defiled; that there be no immoral or godless person like Esau, who sold his own birthright for a single meal. For you know that even afterwards, when he desired to inherit the blessing, he was rejected, for he found no place for repentance, though he sought for it with tears.*
>
> Hebrews 12:15-17

What a tragedy! What lack of insight!

It is not always easy to live in this world without being influenced by this world's perspective. In order to fulfill our mission, it is necessary for us to be in the world. God has ordained, however, that we not be *of the world*.

> *I have given them Thy word; and the world has hated them, because they are not of the world, even as I am not of the world. I do not ask Thee to take them out of the world, but to keep them from the evil one. They are not of the world, even as I am not of the world.*
>
> John 17:14-16

The work of the enemy of our souls is to see that this world exerts its influence over us and that we also become *of the world*. When we lose God's perspective and begin thinking in earthly terms, we become short-sighted and can easily give up eternal riches in exchange for temporal trinkets.

With the loss of perspective comes the loss of power to perform the task that God has entrusted into our hands. If you are just another person, like any other person who lives here on the earth, what do you have to offer people? Nothing!

It is because of this loss of perspective that the Christian message often deteriorates into a very different gospel. When we begin to tell people just to be better citizens, to pay their bills, and not to beat their wives, we have nothing more to offer than other religions.

The Christian message is totally unique. It is "other-worldly." If your life is not consistent with the message you preach, your message will go unheeded. If your perspective is not consistent with the message you preach, you become a hypocrite to the whole world.

The battle we face with humanism today is a fierce one. Long ago the humanists declared plainly in their manifestoes that their goal was to make humanism America's new religion. Humanism is the declared enemy of Christianity and has vowed to rid our school system and our American family life of Divine influence.

Humanism declares that life may be controlled through man's reason, that reason is the highest form of intellect, and that reasonable people will work together to make this world a better place to live. The influence of humanism on our public school system and its insistence on individualism, as opposed to family and community, had left an indelible mark on our young people and become the greatest contributor to teenage suicide today. Young people, in learning to be self-reliant, have become isolated and lonely and desperate.

God's Word teaches something diametrically opposed to these teachings:

> *Trust in the Lord with all thine heart; and lean not unto thine own understanding. In all thy ways acknowledge him, and he shall direct thy paths.*
>
> Proverbs 3:5-6, KJV

Which philosophy do you choose? What is your perspective on life?

Chapter Three

The Proper Attitude

*Have this attitude in yourselves which was also in Christ
Jesus,*

Philippians 2:5

When you have heavenly perspective, you develop a
proper attitude, a Christ-like attitude. I didn't fully realize
the importance of attitude until I began to fly a plane. (I fly
only on my computer. It's safer that way. When I do crash, I
just reboot and fly off again. It is much less expensive—in
every sense of the word.)

According to Webster, *attitude* is an aeronautical term that
signifies *the position of an aircraft in relation to a given point of
reference, usually on the ground level.* A plane can be pointed
northeast but actually be flying north. When that happens,
its attitude is wrong. If the plane continues to fly in that way,
it is in danger of being torn apart by the pressures exerted on
it. The attitude of that plane must be corrected. It must get
pointed in the right direction.

A lot of Christian people need attitude adjustments these
days. They are heading in the wrong direction. They will not
prosper for long. The pressure built up by knowing the will

of God but heading away from it, because of a faulty attitude, will inevitably cause shipwreck—unless that attitude is corrected in time.

When your aeronautical attitude is wrong, it is impossible to see clearly where you are going. In the same way, if you get your spiritual attitude straightened out, I promise that you will see things much more clearly.

How can we develop the attitude *which was also in Christ Jesus*? The Word of God is able to renew us to a mental state that is pleasing to our heavenly Father.

> *And do not be conformed to this world, but be transformed by the renewing of your mind, that you may prove what the will of God is, that which is good and acceptable and perfect.*
>
> Romans 12:2

Those who *received the word with great eagerness* are called by Scripture *noble-minded* (Acts 17:11). Those who didn't were called *fools* (Luke 24:25). Which will you be?

The promise of a changed attitude in our way of thinking is part of the Old Testament promise of salvation. Hebrews repeats the promise recorded in Jeremiah.

> *For this is the covenant that I will make with the house of Israel. After those days, says the Lord: I will put My laws into their minds, And I will write them upon their hearts. And I will be their God, And they shall be My people.*
>
> Hebrews 8:10

What a glorious promise!

Don't hesitate! Time is of the essence! Get an attitude adjustment today.

Chapter Four

Unbelieving Believers

Then the disciples came to Jesus privately and said, "Why could we not cast it out?"

And He said to them, "Because of the littleness of your faith; for truly I say to you, if you have faith as a mustard seed, you shall say to this mountain, 'Move from here to there,' and it shall move; and nothing shall be impossible TO YOU."

Matthew 17:19-20

We have entirely too many unbelieving believers in our ranks today. I know that this is a contradiction of terms, but let me explain what I mean. I call them "unbelieving believers" because: Even though they are saved and have had an experience with God, at some point they stopped believing that God would work for them. Their faith is no longer active. They no longer believe that God is intervening in their daily affairs. Because of that they do not act on their faith. True faith is not just confessed, it is performed, as well.

These people couldn't tell you for sure if they are in the will of God or not. They believe in God, but they have lost that personal reliance on Him.

It isn't difficult to see how this happens. When you have experienced a few setbacks and the devil has you down, he doesn't let you rest. He is not known for conducting a fair fight. While you are down, he continues to pummel you relentlessly.

It takes a very positive attitude in those moments to know that God is still on your side and that you are destined to win, even if the enemy has taken the last round.

When we keep our attitudes straight and keep our faith active, we can maintain our proper identity. All the forces of hell cannot overcome a child of God who knows that his identity is linked to the eternal, not to the temporal.

We are the children of God. We are not the product of circumstances. We are divinely ordained and destined for greatness in our Father's eternal Kingdom.

We are not just bumping along through life, suffering the results of our choices. We are walking a pre-ordained path. The One who ordained our lives has all wisdom and knowledge. We can trust His choices. His Word declares:

But IN ALL THESE THINGS we overwhelmingly conquer through Him who loved us.

Romans 8:37

I can do ALL THINGS through Him who strengthens me.
Philippians 4:13

God has declared my identity. My attitude, my faith must be in line with what He has said. When I believe what God says about me, I succeed every time. My success does not depend on my past performance. It depends on His Word and my faith in His Word.

Don't lose sight of His promises, even when the enemy has you down for the count. You are victorious in Christ. Keep your faith active. Don't let it be moved by circumstances. Our God never fails us.

Chapter Five

Further Development of Our Alien Identity

but speaking the truth in love we are to grow up in all aspects into Him, who is the head, even Christ,

Ephesians 4:15

but grow in the grace and knowledge of our Lord and Savior Jesus Christ....

2 Peter 3:18

Not only should we maintain our identity as aliens in this world; we should constantly grow in that identity. We are not called just to "hold the fort." We must go on to a greater understanding of who we are and what our privileges are in the Lord.

Because we are in this world, there are always traces of this world's nature upon us. We must strive to further develop our alien nature and become less and less a part of this world's system.

Most Christians do exactly the opposite. When they are born again, they make some radical changes and separate themselves from the world in significant ways. As time goes by, however, they are tempted to drop the differences and relate more and more to the people around them: family members, friends, and business associates. The distinctions grow less and less, until there are no distinctions at all. These people have returned to the world.

God has called us to be more and more alien as time goes on, to be more and more like Jesus. We must never grow comfortable with this world. As we get nearer to Heaven, a desire for heavenly things should take hold of us as never before. Christians who seem to have an insatiable lust for the things they feel they have been missing in life always end in double tragedy, for they not only hurt themselves, but other people around them as well.

When we maintain our alien identity, other people see it and have a goal to work toward. When we compromise, however, all lines of distinction are smudged, and confusion results. We not only hurt ourselves, we hurt others who look to us for guidance and example.

If you are becoming too comfortable with this world, that fact should be a matter of alarm, not of joy and rejoicing. We don't belong here. This world is not our home. We cannot be comfortable here. We are displaced aliens.

Much of the message being presented these days as "Christian" leads us to be at ease in the midst of a *crooked and perverse generation*. We are told that God will provide our every need so that we will never feel discomfort or have to struggle to exist in this world. We are told that when we do experience struggles, we can always overcome them, and things will always turn out well for us.

Jesus said:

It is enough for the disciple that he become as his teacher, and the slave as his master. If they have called the head of the house Beelzebul, how much more the members of his household!

Matthew 10:25

If things did not go well for Jesus in this world, how can we expect our lives to be different? He is the teacher; we are the disciples. He is the master; we are His love slaves.

The message we are receiving these days leads us to believe that our situation in this world is rather permanent. We are led to believe that we will reach perfection here as superior beings. The fact that we are transients and are only passing through this world has been all but lost.

While preachers are telling us that we should be experiencing less problems as we grow in God, my experience is the opposite. The more I become like Jesus, the more this world hates me, and the more my problems increase.

Just as our identity must be based on what God says about us and not on what we think about ourselves, the progress of our faith, the development of our spiritual identity, must be based totally on His Word, not on popular precepts.

You are not who you decide to be. You are who God makes you. You are not what you feel like being. You may feel wonderful and still fail miserably. Your identity, present and future, is wrapped up totally in His truth.

The local church must correct her posture before the world and present herself for what she really is, an alien light in this dark world. Recognize your true identity and you will have taken a giant step toward victory in your Christian life, as well.

Part II

The Local Church:

Her Purpose

Chapter Six

The Two-Fold Mission

To me, the very least of all saints, this grace was given, to preach to the Gentiles the unfathomable riches of Christ, and to bring to light what is the administration of the mystery which for ages has been hidden in God, who created all things; in order that the manifold wisdom of God might now be made known through the church to the rulers and the authorities in the heavenly places. This was in accordance with the eternal purpose which He carried out in Christ Jesus our Lord, in whom we have boldness and confident access through faith in Him.

Ephesians 3:8-12

Paul had a mission and a God-given grace to accomplish that mission. That same grace is available to all of God's children today. We need it, for a great two-fold mission has been entrusted to us.

We have a reason for living. We have a purpose in life. When things get difficult, some people come to believe that their only task in life is to "make it to the end." Just getting through the day is a victory for them. But our goal is not just survival. We are here for a purpose. We have something important to accomplish in life.

A mission is a vision put into action. Our vision is God-inspired. It is not fleshly. It is not carnal. It is divine.

Our mission is directly tied to our identity. We are not of this world, so our mission is other-worldly. We are pilgrims and strangers here, so our vision is not limited by the frailties of human short-sightedness. Our mission is God's mission.

Many Christians have lost their mission in life. This may be because they have lost their identity. When we lose sight of our alien nature, we quickly lose sight of our unique mission as well.

During World War II, Jews who were forced into concentration camps in one of the Baltic countries were expected to refine gasoline and motor oil for the Nazis. They tried every way they could to slow the process and to sabotage the refinery.

To punish them, their Nazi commandant lined them up in two groups facing opposing sides of the camp. Those on one side were forced to fill sacks with dirt, carry the sacks to the other side, and empty them. The other group loaded up the same dirt, carried it back to the other side, and dumped it—thus creating an endless and useless task. In only two weeks, the spirit of the prisoners was broken. The commandant had taken away their reason for existence, and they began to show signs of mental collapse.

We have a unique reason for living. If we do not fulfill that unique mission, we have no right to exist as a church, and we are in danger of collapse.

We are all familiar with the English fox hunt:

What a glorious sight it is. The men and their horses are both arrayed in hunting finery. And their dogs, the fox hounds, are ready to lead the chase.

I find those dogs, specially trained for the fox hunt, to be so interesting. When I was in England some years ago, a man told me about their training. Only one of the hounds is actually trained to catch the scent and sight of the fox and to lead the others. The rest just follow along, barking away. What a sight they make: eyes glazed, mouths foaming, tongues wagging; and they don't even understand what they are doing. They are just following the leader.

When I heard that, I had a mental picture of a lot of Christians I know. Somehow I get the impression that many people are running in this Christian race, getting excited, and actually praising God—while, at the same time, they are unsure of what it is all about. Most of us have never yet seen the fox. We are just going on someone else's word. No wonder they easily lose interest and fall by the wayside! Few people can persevere without a clear picture of what they are striving for. Everyone needs a vision and a mission in life.

What does God want us to do?

Are we just here killing time until eternity begins?

What is the purpose of this race?

What is our goal?

Why are we here?

We have a two-fold mission: (1) We are placed here as shining lights in a dark world, and (2) we are called to prove what Paul meant, when he said:

...CHRIST IN YOU, the hope of glory.

Colossians 1:27

Jesus expressed this two-fold mission in another way:

But the one who endures to the end, he shall be saved. And this gospel of the kingdom shall be preached in the whole world for a witness to all the nations, and then the end shall come.

Matthew 24:13-14

1. Our first mission is to endure and see that others endure to the end.

2. Our second mission is to preach the gospel in the whole world.

These two goals are not disparate or divergent. They complement each other. They are one and the same. In order to go to the ends of the earth, we must become like Jesus. In order to present the heavenly message, we must learn to live the heavenly life. In order to be examples of what we preach, we must first experience it in our own lives. We have a two-fold mission.

Chapter Seven

Reaching Out to the Whole World

And this gospel of the kingdom shall be preached in the whole world for a witness to all the nations, and then the end shall come.

Matthew 24:14

I find this to be the only definite statement in scripture concerning the timing of the end. Many people speculate about the timing. They draw charts and graphs and try to match prophecies (given in diverse times and places) in order to come up with tentative dates. But here is a definite fact: *This gospel of the kingdom shall be preached in the whole world, and then the end shall come.*

This is not speculation. Those who are looking for the end should be looking for the gospel to be preached in all nations or to all people. Jesus is concerned about all the people of the earth. He loves all men everywhere. He wants to save all people. He wants His message of mercy and grace to be preached everywhere. And He has given us the privilege of participating in the vision of His heart.

There are several important things that we should note about this passage:

1. It is *the gospel of the kingdom* that will be preached.

2. It will be preached as a witness.

(This is a powerful word, especially when we look at anthropology and the cultural aspect of reaching people.)

3. It shall be preached to *all the nations [or peoples] of the earth.*

(It is estimated that there are more than twenty-two thousand people-groups existing who have never yet received a valid gospel witness—meaning a witness in terms that are relevant to them personally.)

We have a great mission. The Lord has called us to preach His glorious gospel. Our mission has no boundaries. We are to go to the ends of the earth.

Our mission begins with our neighbors, with the people who live on our street, with the people with whom we come in contact in the work place, in our place of study, and in our children's school. But our mission doesn't stop there. It is universal, to all nations, to all peoples.

God has ordained that we become His body, His reflection to the world. We were not planted here simply as another group of "do-gooders." We are the revelation of God through Christ to the world. That is the vision which God has imparted to His people.

Because Jesus is not here in a physical sense, the Church is to reveal Jesus to the world. Jesus said to His disciples:

> *But I tell you the truth, it is to your advantage that I go away; for if I do not go away, the Helper shall not come to you; but if I go, I will send Him to you.*
>
> John 16:7

The disciples could not understand how it would possibly be better for them if Jesus went away. They couldn't bear the thought of His departure. They would be lost without Him. He had been with them almost constantly for three and a half years. During that time, every demon He had spoken to had obeyed His voice and come out of those who were afflicted with them. Every sick person He had touched was healed. He had fed those who were hungry, and food was left over to take home. How was it possible that they would be better off without Him?

The disciples were looking at the matter strictly in a physical sense. They didn't want to lose the presence of Jesus. That is understandable. But He had a greater plan. They wouldn't lose His presence. He would still be with them. Now, however, their privilege would be greater. He would be *in* them, as well.

He did not call a group of people to learn Christian principles. He called a group of people through whom He could live His life to the world. He did not stop delivering people from demons; He does that now through His people. He did not stop healing the sick; He does that now through His people. He called us to be His hands, His feet, His Body.

We are not the result of Jesus having founded a new religion. We are the result of God's desire to live His life through the church. This is God's vision. This is our mission.

There is no plan "B." There is no backup strategy. This is it. God is preparing a people who will express His life to the world. Period!

I have to admit that I don't know the particulars. I don't know how God will accomplish His strategy. But I know that this is His plan.

The will of God is not some deep, dark secret. It is not even difficult to understand. It does not take a cunning person to perceive it. God is looking for obedient people who will move at His direction to show Himself to the world.

He will use anyone. The fact that He uses me is proof of that fact. All that He requires is that we let Him be God.

You have tried to be god of your life and failed. Let Him be God now. He knows how to be God. Even on the bad days, He knows what He is doing. He made everything. He formed every thought and every concept. Leave it all to Him. He is God. Let Him be God.

Our mission, in very simple terms, is to bring Him (through us) to the nations. Make that mission the center of your life. Without it, you lose your unique reason for existing.

Chapter Eight

Becoming Like Jesus

But the one who endures to the end, he shall be saved.

Matthew 24:13

The evangelistic part of our mission cannot be fulfilled without the other essential element—becoming like Jesus. We cannot be lights to the world if we have no light to share. We cannot take God's message to mankind if we are not His unique people, in whom and through whom He lives.

We are called to become Christ-like. That is my personal goal in life. That should be the goal of every man, woman, boy and girl. I am not striving to learn to do what Jesus does. I am striving to let Him live His life through me. His power is not manifested through my being able to mimic what He does. His power is manifested as His character is revealed in me.

John the Baptist knew the secret of having God's power revealed in His life. He said:

He must increase, but I must decrease.

John 3:30

Another way of saying it would be: in order for Him to increase, I must decrease. The victorious life is learning to be selfless, to let Christ dominate my life, to let Him be the center of attention. It is learning to lose my life for His sake. When I do that, I find true life.

The world is desperately searching for life. Our young people are being taught that they must assert themselves and aggressively go after life. Jesus taught just the opposite.

He who has found his life shall lose it, and he who has lost his life for My sake shall find it.

Matthew 10:39

In order to be like Jesus, we must see ourselves, first, as dead with Him; secondly, we must see Him alive in us and living through us. Then, we see that becoming Christ-like naturally leads to reaching out to people around us.

When the Church takes on the character of Christ and becomes selfless in its walk with Him, the ends of the earth become our natural calling. Those who are lining up in missions' offices are people who are willing to lay down their lives for the gospel. They are selfless. They are Christ-like.

If you want to reach to the ends of the earth, you have to become Christ-like. This is His burden. This is His vision. This is our mission.

In order to go to the ends of the earth, we must become selfless. Selfish people don't often have a desire to become missionaries. People whose goal is to become rich don't often volunteer for service to others. Those who want to be waited on, who have a yearning for power and prestige, seek other positions in life.

Selfish people don't want to obey God. As Paul taught:

For the mind set on the flesh is death, but the mind set on the Spirit is life and peace, because the mind set on the flesh is hostile toward God; for it does not subject itself to the law of God, for it is not even able to do so; and those who are in the flesh cannot please God.

Romans 8:6-8

The flesh does not want to do God's will. It is not compliant and cooperative. It is impossible to obey God in the flesh. The flesh must be crucified, and Christ must reign in our hearts.

When Jesus lives in us, we love the people of the world—because He loves all the people of the world. When Jesus lives in us, we become givers—because He is a giver. When Jesus lives in us, we have a burden for those who don't know Him. This is His burden.

Becoming Christ-like does not happen automatically, without any effort on our part. There is a maturing process. It is because of the need to mature into the image of Christ that God has placed special ministries in the church, making our task far more than evangelistic in nature.

And He gave some as apostles, and some as prophets, and some as evangelists, and some as pastors and teachers, for the equipping of the saints for the work of service, to the building up of the body of Christ; until we all attain to the unity of the faith, and of the knowledge of the Son of God, to a mature man, to the measure of the stature which belongs to the fulness of Christ.

As a result, we are no longer to be children, tossed here and there by waves, and carried about by every wind of doctrine, by the trickery of men, by craftiness in deceitful scheming; but speaking the truth in love, we are to grow up in all aspects into Him, who is the head, even Christ, from whom the whole body, being fitted and held together by that which every joint supplies, according to the proper working of each individual part, causes the growth of the body for the building up of itself in love.

Ephesians 4:11-16

Our Heavenly Father doesn't leave newborn babes to fend for themselves. His will for every one of His children is that together they grow into the measure of the stature of the fullness of Christ. That is saying a lot. That is like trying to pour the contents of a five gallon container into a one-ounce glass. It simply cannot be done. We cannot contain all that Christ is!

Here in America, our electrical system operates on 110 volts. Many other countries have higher voltage—220 volts or more. Plugging a 110 volt appliance into a 220 volt line results in the quick destruction of the appliance involved. It can't handle all that power.

Taking on the fullness of Christ is like putting 20,000 volts into a normal American appliance. It couldn't handle it, and we can't handle it either. If Jesus tried to express Himself through us in His fullness, He would blow all of our circuits. We could not contain Him. Our limited capacity could not express adequately His beauty, His power, or His worth.

Thank God He knows what we can contain. He knows what we can handle. He knows how much to express Himself through us at any given time.

But God's will is for us to grow quickly, to increase our capacity quickly, so that we can express to the world His fullness. (As individuals, we could never express His fullness, but as a Body, we can.) This growing process requires discipleship. It requires pastoral care. It requires community effort. We are not striving just to feel good about ourselves. We are striving to expand our borders so that God can express Himself more fully through us.

In order for us to be perfected, we need the ministries that God has place in the Church: the ministry of apostles, the ministry of prophets, the ministry of evangelists, and the ministry of pastors and teachers. These ministries can help us to grow into the measure of the stature of the fullness of Christ. Therefore, they must be recognized and activated.

The church is desperately in need of ministers who are apostolic, prophetic, evangelistic and pastoral. God has promised to place these giftings into the Church. We must recognize them and give place to their operation.

Chapter Nine

The Ministry of Apostles

And at the hands of the APOSTLES many signs and wonders were taking place among the people;...

Acts 5:12

Now when Simon saw that the Spirit was bestowed through the laying on of the APOSTLES' hands, he offered them money,

Acts 8:18

And the APOSTLES and the elders came together to look into this matter.

Acts 15:6

An apostle is one whose burden is the planting of churches. He lays foundations. Those who receive this special anointing have a burden for the whole earth. Their delight is to see the gospel preached in new places. They have the grace to lay the proper foundations for the advancement of a new church.

Paul was a wonderful example. He went to many places and preached the gospel for the first time. As a result, new churches were planted. Whole communities of God's people were raised up and became witnesses to their respective areas.

Paul did his work well:

And this took place for two years, so that all who lived in Asia heard the word of the Lord, both Jews and Greeks.

Acts 19:10

All the credit cannot go to the Apostle Paul, however. He didn't preach to everyone. He established other ministries in each place. The Church, as a whole, preached to everyone. He imparted his burden for the lost to those to whom he ministered. Every apostle should leave the churches he plants with a world-wide vision.

The New Testament speaks more of apostles than any other Ephesians four gifts. Though today, the ministry of apostles is not widely recognized. For the church to be correctly built, it needs the ministry of the wise master-builders.

In some circles the apostolic ministry is being recognized and we are seeing the advantage of built churches and also of networking of apostolic spheres bringing additional growth to the church at large.

Chapter Ten

The Ministry of Prophets

"Of Him all the prophets bear witness...

Acts 10:43

Prophets speak on God's behalf. The prophets of the Old Testament were raised up during periods of disorientation and apostasy among God's people. They spoke on God's behalf and called the people back to their Creator.

But the ministry of prophets did not end with the Old Testament. There were prophets present in the early church.

Now at this time some PROPHETS came down from Jerusalem to Antioch.

Acts 11:27

Now there were at Antioch, in the church that was there, PROPHETS and teachers:...

Acts 13:1

And Judas and Silas, also being PROPHETS themselves, encouraged and strengthened the brethren with a lengthy message.

Acts 15:32

*And as we were staying there for some days, a certain
PROPHET named Agabus came down from Judea.*

Acts 21:10

Prophets call us back to a proper perspective. They call us
to come face to face with God Himself. When we have lost
that heavenly perspective and have turned from God,
prophets arise to call us back and show us that we are pointed
in the wrong direction, that we have a wrong attitude.

The prophetic ministry gives us a sense of right and
wrong. It stands for righteousness and justice, hates injustice
and prejudice. Though many view the prophetic ministry
warily it is much needed today.

The New Testament shows apostles and prophets working
together laying foundations and bringing order to churches.
It was the prophetic which brought special revelation at times
to help direct the church.

The ministry of prophets is experiencing a resurgence in
the Church today. We desperately need the presence of those
who carry a genuine message directly from the throne of
God.

Chapter Eleven

The Ministry of Evangelists

And on the next day we departed and came to Caesarea; and entering the house of Philip the EVANGELIST, who was one of the seven, we stayed with him.

Acts 21:8

But you, be sober in all things, endure hardship, do the work of an evangelist, fulfill your ministry.

2 Timothy 4:5

Evangelists obviously evangelize, but they do much more. They equip the Church to evangelize. They convey to the whole Church a burden for the lost and help us not to see the lost as a burden. They impart the compassion of Christ. Churches that have been blessed by the ministry of a competent and anointed evangelist are fired up to win souls.

When we have the spirit of the evangelist, we begin to see people as God sees them, and we know that with His help we can win them from sin to salvation. We see the lost as victims rather than as perpetrators, as those who are sinned against rather than as those who promote sin.

A friend of mine worked as a missionary in Korea, witnessing to the prostitutes who gathered around the American military bases. During his first year there, he didn't have much success. One reason was that he was still learning the language. The other reason was that he looked upon those prostitutes as people deserving the wrath of God. He was determined to warn them that they were on a straight path toward hell. No wonder he didn't have a single convert that first year!

One morning, while he was having breakfast, God told him to go to the bus station. At the bus station, he noticed that many young people were getting off the buses. He inquired and found that they were coming from the countryside to the big city, looking for work. He noticed that many of these young people seemed to be disoriented, not knowing exactly where to go or what to do. Then he noticed the pimps. They were taking advantage of the situation and trying to con the young country girls into going with them. They would put them into impossible situations, leading them to eventually become prostitutes for the sake of survival.

Next the Lord spoke to him to meet one of the prostitutes and talk to her at length, asking questions about how and why she was in that position. She described to him exactly what he had witnessed at the bus station.

From that day on, my friend had a different attitude about the girls he was sent to witness to. He saw them as victims of deceit. They were innocent country girls, looking for work, not filthy prostitutes. His heart went out to them in genuine compassion.

Needless to say, his ministry changed radically, and he had much fruit to show for his efforts.

A true evangelist sees people as God sees them.

Chapter Twelve

The Ministry of Pastor / Teachers

Be on guard for yourselves and for all the flock, among which the Holy Spirit has made you overseers, to SHEPHERD the church of God which He purchased with His own blood.

Acts 20:28

SHEPHERD the flock of God among you, exercising oversight...

1 Peter 5:2

And every day, in the temple and from house to house, they kept right on TEACHING and preaching Jesus as the Christ.

Acts 5:42

Now there were at Antioch, in the church that was there, prophets and TEACHERS:...

Acts 13:1

And he settled there a year and six months, teaching the word of God among them.

Acts 18:11

Although Ephesians refers to *pastors and teachers*, I believe that this is one gift, not two separate gifts. A more correct rendering of the text would be *pastors who are teachers*. I would call it the ministry of pastor/teachers.

Teachers are those who have the God-given ability to take the Word of God, make it into bite-size pieces that apply to the existing conditions in which believers find themselves, and effectively feed it to them. They teach men and women how to practically perform the will of God in their daily lives. They teach them how to be a whole person, a whole believer. They teach them how to respond to God, how to be obedient to Him. They teach them how to be disciplined.

Teachers show their care for believers through the act of feeding them the life-giving Word. What could be more important to any of us? It is what God has said to us that keeps us strong and going forward in our Christian life. His Word is life. Teachers are able to help us understand what God is saying to us at any given time.

This ministry takes great patience. Christians don't pop up like warm bread from the toaster. It takes time and much patient teaching to mature God's people. The apostles taught *every day* and *from house to house*. They were sure to systematically lay a foundation of truth in the life of each new believer. This is the role of the pastor/teacher.

These ministries overlap. Every minister must have a pastoral burden. An apostle must have both an evangelistic and a pastoral spirit. Prophets must have the heart of a care giver, as well. Even evangelists must be pastoral. Every minister of God must be ready to lay down his life down for the sheep.

If we are to do the will of God, we must receive the ministry gifts as God raises them up or brings them into our midst.

Chapter Thirteen

The Balanced Mission

Woe to you, scribes and Pharisees, hypocrites! For you tithe mint and dill and cummin, and have neglected the weightier provisions of the law: justice and mercy and faithfulness; but THESE ARE THE THINGS YOU SHOULD HAVE DONE WITHOUT NEGLECTING THE OTHERS.

Matthew 23:23

The two things that God wants to do for us are: (1) to make us more like Jesus and (2) to send us to the ends of the earth to proclaim His love and reveal Himself through us to the world. If you read the Bible with these two thoughts in mind, everything will take on new meaning for you.

Many churches go off to one extreme or the other of this two-fold mission. Some churches make a great effort to reach out to the unsaved, all the while neglecting to care for the flock. Some very missions-conscious churches seem to be oblivious of the fact that they have serious problems at home. When families are being destroyed and saints are falling into serious sin, we need to give more attention to the flock over which God has placed us.

On the other hand, many churches get so involved in their inner workings that they totally forget about preaching the

Gospel to the unsaved. The fact that someone needs to hear the Gospel almost seems to be an intrusion to them. They don't have time for that. They are too busy "building the church."

We must maintain a proper balance, caring for the flock and reaching out to the world around us. The two are inter-dependent. Without a strong flock, how can we reach out? And unless we win others, who will reach out to new areas?

An imbalance in either direction is not to our advantage. Although it is not wrong to be strong in one particular area of ministry we must remember the words of Jesus:

THESE ARE THE THINGS YOU SHOULD HAVE DONE WITHOUT NEGLECTING THE OTHERS.

Every church should work toward a balance of mission. A church without a worldwide vision cannot grow to its full potential; and a church without strong pastoral guidance will eventually founder on the rocks.

Our ultimate goal should be that which interests Jesus. He said that when we had preached the Gospel to all the nations: "*then the end will come*" (Matthew 24:14). He is interested in "*the end*." We should also be interested in "*the end*." As God's people, we must bear His vision, obey His mission, looking for "*the end*," a time when we will be physically reunited with our heavenly Father and will return Home to live with Him forever.

It is time for the local church to regain her sense of purpose in this world.

Part III

The Local Church:

Her Proclamation

Chapter Fourteen

Kingdom, Not Culture

But sanctify Christ as Lord in your hearts, always being ready to make a defense to everyone who asks you to give an account for the hope that is in you, yet with gentleness and reverence;

1 Peter 3:15

Our mission is expressed in our message, and both are related to our identity. Staying true to our identity permits us to maintain a clear message, which we must then communicate. Communicating the message is our mission. This is the reason we go to the ends of the earth.

Whether we like it or not, each of us has a message. We all stand for something. In some way, for good or for evil, we influence the people we meet. Our message is not always preached in the formal setting. Sometimes we just live the message.

Many Christians carry a confusing message. Because they are not sure about so many things in life, they come across as confused and confusing.

Even if your message is strong and clear, it may be misunderstood. But that is not your fault. Your responsibility is to be ready at any time to defend your faith.

Every believer should be able to make a defense for the hope that is in their hearts. That doesn't mean to be defensive about your Christianity. It means to be able to say what it is that you believe, to be able to communicate your message.

Since we must communicate our message, we should certainly know what that message is. If someone asks you, "What are you so happy about?" you should be able to share the message of the Kingdom with them.

Some missionaries, instead of giving the pure message of the Kingdom, have exported a mixture of Christian teaching and American culture. In a way, that is understandable. We each interpret the gospel in the light of our personal situation. That doesn't mean, however, that everyone in the whole world should apply it in the same way. The secret of effective evangelism is to bring the gospel to others in a way which is meaningful to them—in their particular cultural setting.

The gospel is not American. It is universal. Winning people to Christ doesn't mean converting them to Americans. It means conforming them to the image of Christ.

The kingdom of God is not American. It is universal. It applies to all people in every cultural situation. Jesus is Lord in every nation and among every tribe. The people there may not dress the way I do. They may not eat the same things I do. They may have customs that are very strange to me. Yet Christ is Lord in that place, as much as He is Lord in my hometown. The gospel can reach into any cultural setting and be relevant to the people in that cultural setting.

In his book, *Peace Child*, Don Richardson told of going to New Guinea to share the gospel with headhunters who believed that treachery was life's highest achievement. If they could deceive or kill, even a best friend, they felt fulfilled. The story of how he was eventually able to communicate the gospel to these people is amazing.

God's power can change the most corrupt society. Those primitive tribal people did not need to be westernized, they needed to be Christianized. There is a great difference. Don Richardson was not sent to destroy the culture of the tribes of New Guinea. He was sent to reveal Christ to them—in their own cultural setting.

Although it must be contextualized differently in every cultural setting, our message has certain elements that must always be present if the gospel is to maintain its unique life-changing essence.

Your message may vary with the need of the individual to whom you are ministering; but there are several important components to the message which should remain more or less constant. I want to emphasize several of them.

Chapter Fifteen

The First Necessary Element of Our Message: The King

Again, the kingdom of heaven is like a dragnet cast into the sea, and gathering fish of every kind; and when it was filled, they drew it up on the beach; and they sat down, and gathered the good fish into containers, but the bad they threw away. So shall it be at the end of the age; the angels shall come forth, and take out the wicked from among the righteous, and will cast them into the furnace of fire; there shall be weeping and gnashing of teeth.

Matthew 13:47-50

Our message must contain the King. This is His message. This is His mission. We are His people. Don't leave Him out of the message. Our message is the gospel of the kingdom and the gospel of the King. Gospel means "good news." This is the "good news" of Jesus Christ, the King of Kings.

All of the parables of the New Testament are kingdom parables. They teach us how to respond to the King. This is one of my favorites. That net collects everything in its path. Nothing escapes it. There have been seasons in my life in which I felt I was simply being dragged along by the net. Things were out of my control. The kingdom was moving along, and I was being moved along with it. Fortunately, I am one of the good fish. Thank God that I am on the right side.

The message of the King and His kingdom helps us to put into the proper perspective the current events in the world today. When all is said and done, we know one thing: Jesus is still on the throne. However we feel about the things that are happening in the world, whether we like or dislike the turn of events, we always know WHO is ultimately in control. Jesus is still King.

We didn't like what the Chinese authorities did in Tienamen Square a few years ago. We did like the fall of Communism in eastern Europe and the failure of the hardline coup in the Soviet Union in August of 1991. But, in all of these situations, Jesus is still on the throne. That is the marvel of the Christian message. Nothing that men can do will ever change it. Because He never changes, our message never changes. He is Lord.

The news of the day may not favor our particular political persuasion but, when we are kingdom oriented and not politically oriented, we can always know that everything is under control—because He is still on the throne. Our message is the gospel of the King, and it must be presented as such.

When we present the gospel as a list of do's and don'ts, people get confused. "I don't know if I can live up to that," they say. "I don't know if I can be faithful to that ideal." But that is not the issue. The issue is: **Jesus is Lord. Are you willing to submit to His authority in your life?** Nothing else matters. The gospel is not a list of do's and don'ts. It is submission to the Lordship of Jesus Christ.

Jesus taught:

For which one of you, when he wants to build a tower, does not first sit down and calculate the cost, to see if he has enough to complete it? Otherwise, when he has laid a foundation, and is not able to finish, all who observe it begin to ridicule him, saying, 'This man began to build and was not able to finish.'

Or what king, when he sets out to meet another king in battle, will not first sit down and take counsel whether he is strong enough with ten thousand men to encounter the one coming against him with twenty thousand?

Luke 14:28-31

It is good to count the cost before making a decision to follow Jesus. And the question to be answered is: Are you willing to let Him be Lord of your life? Nothing else.

A gospel without the King is not the gospel at all. Salvation is not just fire insurance. It is not just an inspector's stamp of approval. It is a whole new way of life. It is submission to the will of the King.

If we give people the idea that they can be saved, have their sins forgiven, and then live the way they want to, we are only making them miserable. Obedience to the King cannot be glossed over or watered down. Life without obedience to the King is insanity. Obedience brings sanity.

Many of those who present the Christian message emphasize what you can get out of knowing Christ, what He can do for you. They forget to tell that you must develop a personal relationship with Him. He is not an impersonal king whose throne room is inaccessible. Jesus is a personal King. He is my personal King. He is not only approachable, He requires that we approach Him. Anyone of His subjects may enter His throne room at any time. Anyone of us can reach out and touch Him whenever we need to do so. There is no hierarchy standing in our way. There is no middle management group to bypass. We can go directly to the King.

When people of other religions ask me what is different about mine, I answer, "I know my God personally." Other religions may have a long list of dogmas, but we cut through all that and go directly to the source.

Some of the cults are so well prepared in their verbal arguments that you will have difficulty winning over them in an open discussion. They seem to have all the pat answers. Don't argue with them. Just say, "I know my God. He answers my prayers. He helps me when I am in trouble. He is my friend. I talk to Him every day." And that will end the discussion. Our message is the message of the King.

Chapter Sixteen

The Second Necessary Element of Our Message: New Life

And I shall give them one heart, and shall put a new spirit within them. And I shall take the heart of stone out of their flesh and give them a heart of flesh, that they may walk in My statutes and keep My ordinances, and do them. Then they will be My people, and I will be their God.

Ezekiel 11:19-20

Our message is a message of new life in Christ. God promised through the Prophet Ezekiel to take out the stony heart from His people and replace it with a heart of flesh.

I have new life based on the covenant of God in Christ. My new life is not based on how much I wanted it or how much I tried to have it. Getting that fact into my head and into my heart does wonders for my faith.

I am a new person in Jesus Christ. He put a new heart in me. I can now love people that I would never have been able to love before. I can now hate sin—which I used to love.

Because I am a new person, I can do new things. I have new life in Christ.

This new life did not evolve. I did not get better and better until I became a child of God. This life was created in Christ.

Therefore if anyone is in Christ, he is a new creation; the old has gone, the new has come!

2 Corinthians 5:17, NIV

We are a new creation in Christ.

A frog changes from an egg to a tadpole to a mature frog. If that tadpole could suddenly change into a canary, it might be similar to my new life, which is totally different. I am not a product of evolution. I am a new creation.

In the original language, that word *creation* means *species*. You are a new species. You have not evolved from a lower order. You are a different kind of human altogether, and you must be a representative of that new life.

When we are born again, we come into a new family. Our message contains not only new life, but community life. As a member of a family, we have new relationships. There are other people involved here. We have a common Father. In our new life, we must learn our proper relationship one to another. Within the confines of the Gospel, we must deal with one another as Christians.

Not only do we have a common Father; we have a common experience. We should be able to love each other as brothers and sisters, to forgive each other and to have fellowship with each other. We should be ready to lay down our lives for one another, serving one another willingly and joyfully.

Nearly fifty passages in the New Testament epistles speak of the ministry we are to have ONE TO ANOTHER. For example:

...love ONE ANOTHER;...

Romans 13:8

...accept ONE ANOTHER,....

Romans 15:7

...have the same care for ONE ANOTHER.
1 Corinthians 12:25

Bear ONE ANOTHER'S burdens,....

Galatians 6:2

...show forbearance to ONE ANOTHER in love,
Ephesians 4:2

And be kind to ONE ANOTHER, tenderhearted, forgiving EACH ANOTHER,....

Ephesians 4:32

bearing with ONE ANOTHER, and forgiving EACH OTHER,...just as the Lord forgave you,....
Colossians 3:13

...teaching and admonishing ONE ANOTHER....
Colossians 3:16

Therefore comfort ONE ANOTHER with these words.
1 Thessalonians 4:18

Therefore encourage ONE ANOTHER, and build up ONE ANOTHER,....

1 Thessalonians 5:11

...pray for ONE ANOTHER,....

James 5:16

It is clear that we have a responsibility to each other. Our new life in Christ demands a proper relationship with His entire family.

A gospel without new life is not a gospel at all. Get new life into your message.

Chapter Seventeen

The Third Necessary Element of Our Message: Forgiveness

I, even I, am the one who wipes out your transgressions for My own sake; And I will not remember your sins.

Isaiah 43:25

...,"for I will forgive their iniquity, and their sin I will remember no more."

Jeremiah 31:34

Our God is a God of forgiveness. He is lavish in His forgiveness. His forgiveness is a very large measure of His grace.

I have personally experienced that forgiveness. God has forgiven me; God forgives me; and God will continue to forgive me. He has forgiven me of every bad thing I did in the past. He has forgiven me of every bad thing I tried to do and failed. He has forgiven me of every bad thought I ever had. And, although I do not understand how it can be true, He has forgotten all my sins.

In human terms, God does not see my sin anymore. When He looks at me, He looks through Jesus and only sees His sinless perfection. When God looks at me, He sees the impeccable, pure, and perfect life of Jesus. He does not see my sin. That is divine forgiveness. He has fulfilled the promise given through the prophets Isaiah and Jeremiah.

These promises were remembered in New Testament times:

> *For I will be merciful to their iniquities, and I will remember their sins no more.*
>
> Hebrews 8:12

> *And their sins and their lawless deeds I will remember no more.*
>
> Hebrews 10:17

What a miracle! My sins have been buried in the sea of God's forgetfulness. And God will never go to the sea and dig them up again. He is bound by His covenant. Forgiveness through the blood of Jesus is final.

People often lose patience with one another. And when they get tired of one another, they bring up all the things of the past that serve their purpose and rehash them one by one. God will never do that. He has promised:

> *As far as the east is from the west, So far has He removed our transgressions from us.*
>
> Psalms 103:12

It is noteworthy that He did not say "as far as the north is from the south." Distances between the North and the South can be measured. There is a definite North Pole and a definite South Pole. But where is the West Pole? Or where is the East Pole? West and east are relative terms, depending on where you are at the time. You can always go further east or further west. God meant that His removal of our sin is limitless.

He forgives my failures that I bring to Him today, and He will forgive my failures that I bring to Him tomorrow. That doesn't mean that I try to see how far I can push my luck and still remain in His good graces. I am not trying to see how much I can get away with. I love Him, and I want to please Him. I am not trying to ride on the edge, as far away from Him as possible without toppling over the precipice. To the contrary, I am trying to stay as close to Him as I can.

His love and His unfailing forgiveness gives me a lot of confidence. I don't have to walk on eggshells through life. I can relax and enjoy life. If I fail, He is forgiving.

I know that Jesus died for my sin. In effect, my sin killed Him. If I hadn't sinned, He would not have had to die. I never delight in sin and have no license to sin. But, if I do sin, He is there to help me—without question.

Those who have worked for me marvel at my willingness to forgive. I must, for I am forgiven. I cannot forget what He has done for me.

It is the forgiving aspect of the Gospel that appeals so much to those who are suffering in their sin. Make your message a message of forgiveness.

Chapter Eighteen

The Fourth Necessary Element of Our Message: Hope

In hope against hope he believed, in order that he might become a father of many nations, according to that which had been spoken, "So shall your descendants be."

Romans 4:18

...we exult in hope of the glory of God.

Romans 5:2

And hope does not disappoint,...

Romans 5:5

Our message contains hope, a truth I believe that we will need a lot more in the future. Life has been pretty good to us Americans. In our case, the word "hope" doesn't seem so important.

The old Negro spirituals spoke much of "hope." No doubt that was because life was pretty miserable for those who were composing those noble hymns. During their lifetime they possessed little of this world's goods: a few pieces of clothing, a leaky shack to call home. Their future here was not very bright. Their only earthly comfort was in their work, what family life they were permitted, their few friends, and their faith.

Hope was very important to the slaves. It was all they had sometimes. They knew that a better day was coming. That was all that kept them alive.

Those who live in a peaceful atmosphere understand little about "hope." Only those who have experienced the ravages of war could understand the powerful appeal of that little word.

Because we know nothing of hope, we are not well acquainted with endurance or perseverance. We do not do well in uncomfortable situations. All we can think about is changing the situation—quickly.

The key words of our technological age are "speed" and "ease." The evolution of the microprocessor has made us impatient with life. We want to speed everything up.

I have a tape recorder on which I can adjust the speed of the playback. It is possible to listen to the tape at twice the speed with which it was recorded. After getting accustomed to that, I want to find the speed control on some people I talk to and set them up a notch.

We have come to expect results here and now. We now cook things in seconds in a microwave oven. We want everything to happen quickly. If we have to struggle with something, we would rather lay it aside and do something else. We can't wait.

This impatience is part of the cause of our present economic woes. We are not willing to suffer any inconvenience. When we vote, therefore, we vote against new taxes and also against cutting any government programs. We want it all—NOW.

Our impatience to have the good life has hurt our families. The absence of mothers in the home has had a very detrimental effect upon children. I don't believe, however, that the rise of women in the work place is just a result of women wanting to be "liberated." They are working because we want the money they can earn to sustain our lifestyles. We simply cannot tolerate discomfort these days. We would rather destroy the family than be uncomfortable.

Most of us have no concept of how the poor and oppressed people of the world actually live. How could we possibly understand how important hope is to these people?

Whether we like it or not, all of us have to die at some point, and we need the hope of life after death. Death is a terrible thing to see. There is no dignity in death. Having witnessed the death of both of my parents, I can say with a certainty that human beings were never meant to die. God is not the author of death. Death is the result of sin.

Therefore, just as through one man sin entered into the world, and death through sin, and so death spread to all men, because all sinned—

Romans 5:12

In death, the human body, which once experienced so much glory in this world and through which wonderful sentiments were expressed, is ugly. Robbed of all its glory, it lies motionless and expressionless, except for the pained look of departure.

Thank God for hope. Hope tells us that a day is coming when the dead will live again. Hope tells us that one day life will be different. The banner of God's righteousness will wave from north to south and from east to west; and His justice will prevail.

That new life will not be based on the equity that you have developed in your home or your bank account. It will not be based on your social prestige or your political power. Every facet of that new life will be based on the Lordship of Jesus Christ. And He will reign forever and ever.

In that day, death will be changed into immortality.

But when this perishable will have put on the imperishable, and this mortal will have put on immortality, then will come about the saying that is written, 'Death is swallowed up in victory.'

1 Corinthians 15:54

A gospel without hope is not the true gospel at all. We have the hope of a great future in God.

I would love to live in Montana a couple months out of the year. It is a breath-takingly beautiful place. During the other months, however, I have no desire to be there. It gets so cold that it seems uninhabitable—to me at least.

God has prepared a perfect place for us. I have hope that we will dwell there in safety. I am waiting with great anticipation for this present age to end and a new one to begin. I have hope that when the Lord returns, all will change.

There are two Latin words that we translate "future." One word means the normal progression of events, things that happen, the good with the bad, without outside interference.

The other word comes from the same root as our word "advent." This word shows that God sovereignly intervenes in the affairs of man and imposes His rule upon events.

This concept changes everything. If everything just happens, we have little hope for the future. Or perhaps we have a 50/50 chance of experiencing a good outcome, depending on your point of view. When God is in charge, when He rules over events, we have an assurance that everything will turn out well.

The first advent of Christ into the world totally changed the course of human history. Those of us who know His Word now look forward to His second advent. He will again intrude upon the affairs of man, and everything will change as a result. What a glorious hope! We have nothing to fear.

There are many developments in our world about which we might genuinely be concerned. What polluters are doing to the earth's environment is indeed terrible. We may even see some worse things. Someone may, at some point, detonate nuclear weapons against an enemy nation. I don't believe, however, that the stupidity of man will bring about the end of time. Time will end when God decides it should. He is in charge of the advance of history.

Men who are greedy, immoral, and dishonest will continue to cause suffering in the world. But our God reigns. His second advent will drastically affect the course of future history. When the gospel has been preached as a witness to all the nations, He will return. What a hope!

Don't ever preach a gospel void of hope!

Chapter Nineteen

The Fifth Necessary Element of Our Message: Urgency

And He said to them, "Beware, and be on your guard against every form of greed; for not even when one has an abundance does his life consist of his possessions."

Luke 12:15

Our message must convey a sense of urgency. "Urgency" is usually reserved for "emergencies"; and when we get too comfortable, we lose the sense of urgency associated with life and death issues.

When we have received new life and our situation has improved 100%, it is easy to forget that time is running out for others. Riches have a way of lulling us to sleep, as well. Somehow we consider the poor to be more "in need" than the rich. That isn't necessarily true. Rich people go to hell too. Jesus said life does not consist of *possessions*. Life is not made up of what you collect. Rich people also go to hell.

Somehow we imagine that hell is reserved for strangers. But your friends can go there—if you don't reach them in time. Your children can go there—if you don't reach them in time.

In the poorer countries, emergencies of every nature create a sense of urgency that we have somehow lost in the western world. When thousands of villages have no viable Gospel witness, it is easy for us to see the need of presenting the gospel message. The reality of the situation creates within us an urgency.

In America, however, we have churches on every street corner. Our people hear the gospel on radio and television. Well-known evangelists conduct crusades in every major city. All of this conspires to rob us of a sense of urgency. Yet this is an urgent moment in history. People are dying without Christ. Our children are being destroyed by drugs and immorality. We must return a sense of urgency to our message.

Because most of our American people have heard the gospel in one way or another, our tendency is just to leave them alone and let them make up their own minds about following Christ. This is not God's way. He wants us to be looking for the right moment and the right way to present His Word to each lost soul.

The popular message of the day also contributes to our complacency. We are led to believe that everything will now get better and better until we develop a utopia on earth. What a rude awakening awaits those who accept that teaching at face value!

The Apostle Paul had the benefit of outside influences. Not everything got better for him when he accepted the gospel. Many things got worse. His situation was unstable. He had to learn to be content in whatever state he found himself.

...I have learned to be content in whatever circumstances I am.

Philippians 4:11

Because our circumstances are comfortable, we are complacent. Our complacency troubles the heart of God. If we could see as He sees, we would no longer be complacent. We would feel the urgency of the hour and the need for all people to quickly receive the gospel of Jesus Christ.

Our mission is urgent. It is a matter of life and death. The Holy Spirit is conveying urgency. Our message must convey the same urgency. When Jesus said, *"Beware, and be on your guard,"* He meant exactly what He said.

Chapter Twenty

The Sixth Necessary Element of Our Message: Go

...'You too go into the vineyard, and whatever is right I will give you.' ...

Matthew 20:4

... 'You too go into the vineyard.'

Matthew 20:7

'Go therefore to the main highways, and as many as you find there, invite to the wedding feast.'

Matthew 22:9

'Go therefore and make disciples of all nations, baptizing them in the name of the Father and the Son, and the Holy Spirit,'

Matthew 28:19

Our message contains a "go." We cannot wait for the world to come to us. We have the message all people need. We must take it to them. If they are in the marketplace, if they are in the school systems, or if they are in their own houses, the message must reach them where they are.

Jesus said that we should go to "the ends of the earth." How do we do that? We have to start somewhere. Where do we start?

Jesus said to the disciples:

…*"Follow Me, and I will make you fishers of men."*
Matthew 4:19

Jesus is a Fisher of men too. If we follow Him, He will lead us to fruitful waters. He is going forth to find the lost. Go with Him. Be His instruments.

Go with Jesus, the Master Fisherman. He knows where the fish are receptive. He knows where they are biting. He knows where they are hungry. He knows where they are ready.

Fishing is an art. In some places it is seasonal. You might catch many fish one day (because they are migrating) and another day catch none at all. There are also certain times during the day when fish bite better. There are certain areas where fish like to hide. There are so many factors to take into account: the species, the temperature of the water, the type of bait, etc. Not everyone who throws a line into the water catches a fish.

Go with the Master Fisherman. He knows what He is doing. Follow Him. He will make you fishers of men. He will lead you to people at just the right season in their lives. He will give you just the right bait. He will send you at just the right time of day. With Him, nothing is chance. He has everything planned perfectly.

Going fishing with the Lord demands a lot of flexibility on our part. When a fishing friend calls me to say that the fish are in, I need to know where my fishing tackle is and have it in good condition. Time is of the essence. Sometimes the fish are gone before we get there. The Apostle Paul taught:

…*be ready in season and out of season;….*
2 Timothy 4:2

Be ready with the gospel. Never get too relaxed to go fishing with the Lord. Never get too "out of shape" to be used of Him.

Let there always be a "go" in your message.

The true gospel of the kingdom must, once again, become the proclamation of the local church.

Part IV

The Local Church:

Her Power

Chapter Twenty-one

The Illusive "Power of God"

*And when I came to you, brethren, I did not come with
superiority of speech or of wisdom, proclaiming to you the
testimony of God. For I determined to know nothing among
you except Jesus Christ, and Him crucified. And I was with
you in weakness and in fear and in much trembling. And
my message and my preaching were not in persuasive words
of wisdom, but in demonstration of the Spirit and of power,
that your faith should not rest on the wisdom of men, but
on the power of God.*

1 Corinthians 2:1-5

Too many Christians start out well in this walk, only to
fall along the wayside when trials come their way. Too many
Christians start out with a zeal for the Christian mission and
the Christian message, only to find other interests later in life.
Starting well in this race is not enough. We must also finish
well.

We must learn the secrets of our sustenance, those things
which enable us to maintain our alien identity and to grow
in that identity, those things which empower us to fulfill the
Christian mission and to preach the Christian message.

When Paul went to Corinth, he was facing a sophisticated and corrupt secular society. Yet he turned the city upside down for God. He states here that did not do it with persuasive words of wisdom but with the demonstration of the Spirit and of God's power.

It is no secret that what we need is more of the power of God in our lives. But that power can sometimes be elusive. What is the power of God? And how does it work?

I have experienced the power of God in my life in several different ways. In the following chapters, I want us to investigate the power of the Word of God, the power of the cross and the power of the Holy Spirit.

Chapter Twenty-two

The Power of the Word of God

..."*It is written, 'Man shall not live on bread alone, but on every word that proceeds out of the mouth of God.' "*

Matthew 4:4

The Word of the Lord feeds us. It reminds us of God's plan and will for our lives. It is like a package from home:

When I was sent to Vietnam, I lived as an alien there. I was not born in Vietnam; I am not Vietnamese; and living life as a stranger in a strange place has never been easy. At times I wondered if I would ever see home again.

Occasionally my mother and my sister would spend an evening together, baking my favorite cookies and cakes, and would send them to me. Their packages took up to six weeks to reach me, but they always seemed to arrive at just the right time in my life—when I needed to be reminded that someone loved me and that I had a home to return to one day. Those cookies did so much to remind me that I was an American, with a great heritage and a great future and that I wouldn't be in Vietnam forever. What powerful brownies!

God sends His Word to us to remind us that this world is not our home. He feeds us some morsels of His heavenly fare, reminding us that better things await us—if we fight a good fight and remain faithful to our calling. His Word is bread to the hungry.

The Word of God equips us for whatever lies ahead. It builds us up and strengthens us. It enables us to accomplish the task that God has given to the church. It is a package from home. Savor every divine morsel. This is Heaven's fare. Taste the goodness of Father's table.

In England, I met an American lady who had married an Englishman and settled down there to live. Later, when she tried to contact her large family back home, she couldn't. Somehow she had lost contact with them. This troubled her greatly. Her family was very important to her. Having lost contact with home, she felt very insecure and unstable.

Don't lose touch with home. Don't lose sight of who you are. You have a great heritage. Look for some of those goodies from Father's house. They will remind you of your future. We are not here permanently. This world is not our home.

Christians who wait too long to make contact with home, become disoriented and troubled. Don't take that risk. Keep in touch. Receive God's regular package from home. Feast on His goodness regularly. Don't forget where you came from.

Peter wrote to the first-century Church:

Since you have in obedience to the truth purified your souls for a sincere love of the brethren, fervently love one another from the heart, for you have been born again not of seed which is perishable but imperishable, that is, through the living and abiding word of God.

                                                    1 Peter 1:22-23

We have been born again of seed which Peter calls *the living and abiding word of God*. There is a mystery in the Word of God. It is that God has revealed Himself through His Word. The Word of God is powerful.

Peter went on to say:

For, "All flesh is like grass, and all its glory like the flower of grass. The grass withers, and the flower falls off, but the word of the Lord abides forever." And this is the word which was preached to you.

1 Peter 1:24-25

This Word by which we were born again, abides forever. This seed is eternal.

Seed produces after its own kind. If you plant beans, you reap beans. If you plant tomato seeds, you get tomatoes. You cannot get cucumbers from tomato plants. Good seeds also do not produce weeds. Weeds are produced by weed seeds. Seeds produce their own kind. And this seed is eternal.

When you hold a seed in your hand, you are actually holding the entire plant with its fruit. That total potential abides in the tiny seed. An acorn is a potential oak tree. Everything about that tree is already defined in the seed.

We have been born of a marvelous seed. Unlike the seed of the tomato or the cucumber or the oak tree, this seed is incorruptible. It cannot be perverted. It cannot change. It cannot fail. It cannot disappear. It is the Word of God. When it is planted in your life, it will grow; and it will grow into whatever the Lord has designed for you.

When you were born again, God inscribed in the seed He planted in your heart the particular gifting that He designed for you. The genetics were already there. The total potential of what God ordained for you was in the Word of God planted inside your heart.

Your heavenly Father has designed a marvelous future for you, and God's power will enable you to fulfill your destiny in life. Every detail of your life has already been planned. Nothing is left to chance. You have an eternal purpose. You already are the total of that potential. That seed just needs to grow and develop in you. Water it. Nourish it. Give it every chance to flourish. Achieve your destiny in God.

The people I know who have made the most progress in their Christian experience are those who have allowed God's Word to bear on their lives. There is no other secret formula for growth. These people have not only heard the Word, they have allowed it to work in them.

Too many Christians are kicking against the Word and making excuses as to why they cannot obey it. Too many Christians are rationalizing as to what the Word of God really means in relationship to their lives. Too many cheapen the Word, cut it apart, and try to make it applicable to their lives in a way that they see personally beneficial.

Let the Word of God do what it was meant to do. Stop trying to change it to fit your own desires. The Word of God will never change. All flesh will fade away. The flowers will fade and fall off their stems, but the Word of God will stand forever.

What some people are doing to the Word today is no different from what others have done down through the ages. For thousands of years, those who have not wanted to do God's will have been attempting to destroy the Word of God. Yet their criticisms and rationalizations have not hindered the Word in any way. It stands unchanged. Don't be one of those who waste their time trying to get God to conform to their image. Submit to His will. That is the road to victory in life.

When you rationalize and try to make the Word of God fit your lifestyle, instead of submitting wholly to the will of God, you make the Word of God ineffective in your life. You destroy its power in you. You cannot afford to do that. If you cut your ties to the Word of God, you have cut your ties to home. You are an alien in a foreign world. You cannot live without news from home. Without it, you quickly lose your identity and become a person of the world.

Jesus said:

Therefore take care how you listen; for whoever has, to him shall more be given; and whoever does not have, even what he thinks he has shall be taken away from him.

Luke 8:18

There are parts of the Word that we love, but there are other parts that we are not fond of. We tend to rate the Word of God much like we rate other things around us.

"That verse gets a 10."

"This one rates a 6."

Jesus said, *"Take care how you listen."* Don't take just part of His Word. It is all designed for your growth. Don't grade it or compare it to other things in this world. There is no comparison. Take care how you listen.

Many times we like a particular part of the Word because we like the style of the person who presented it to us. It is not wrong to have favorite speakers. We are free to make those choices. We are not, however, free to reject part of the Word of God simply because we don't like the style of the person who presents it. Our obedience to the Word of God must have nothing to do with personalities.

And for this reason we also constantly thank God that when you received from us the word of God's message, you accepted it not as the word of men, but what it really is, the

*word of God, which also performs its work in you who
believe.*

                                                          1 Thessalonians 2:13

When the Thessalonians listened to Paul speaking the
Word of God, they did not receive it as the message of a man,
but as the message of God. They believed. Therefore the
Word performed its work in them.

The Word of God will change you—if you let it. If you
choose to use the excuse that it came though someone you
don't particularly enjoy hearing, you may miss what God has
destined for your life. The Word is the Word, regardless of
the messenger. A classic example is found in the book of
Hebrews:

*Therefore, let us fear lest, while a promise remains of enter-
ing His rest, any one of you should seem to have come short
of it. For indeed we have had good news preached to us, just
as they also; but the word they heard did not profit them,
because it was not united by faith in those who heard.*

                                                          Hebrews 4:1

These people heard the Word. They had the *good news*
preached to them, yet it did not bear fruit in them. It did not
profit them. It was not "*united by faith.*" They did not accept
it as God's Word. They insisted that it was simply a man's
opinion. Consequently they reaped no benefit from what
they heard.

Several things have conditioned us not to be responsive
to the Word of God these days:

In this age of information, we are bombarded by messages
from every side. It has been estimated that by the time a
person is 21, they have already seen 200,000 commercials.
And it doesn't stop when we reach 21. It keeps multiplying.
After a while, we simply tune out. We barely hear what the

commercial is saying. We have become skeptical, cynical, and distrustful.

If we tire of hearing the Word of God and simply "tune out" to what God is saying, the results can be tragic.

In our educational system, we have been taught to look at everything very scientifically. We are taught to test everything, not to take anything at face value, and to accept only what is proven fact.

Many times, however, the Word of God doesn't seem logical. It certainly is not "scientifically proven" in our understanding of the term. It must be received by faith.

When it is preached, something rings true in our spirits. Our minds may say, "This cannot be." But we feel something in our souls. We sense that this is of God. When we are willing to submit to God's will, we have a sensitive spirit to hear what He says. When we are determined to go our own way, we turn off to what God is saying and the Word of God becomes preposterous to us.

Don't despise this package from home. It is a reminder that we are aliens in this land. Savor every precious morsel. Let it strengthen and fortify you. Let it change you. Water the seed that God has planted in you.

Many consider the Word of God to be restrictive and binding. In reality, it is just the opposite. It is liberating.

Jesus said:

> ..., *"If you abide in My word, then you are truly disciples of Mine; and you shall know the truth, and the truth shall make you free."*

                                                            John 8:31-32

The truth is liberating. The Word of God is truth. It is liberating, not binding. It will free you to act upon your true identity. It will strengthen both your mission and your message. Receive the power of the Word of God for your life.

Chapter Twenty-three

The Power of the Cross

For the word of the cross is to those who are perishing foolishness, but to us who are being saved it is the power of God.

1 Corinthians 1:18

The cross of Jesus Christ is powerful. It releases me to my heavenly identity. It empowers me in my mission and in my message. That is why Paul determined to know nothing among the Corinthians except Jesus Christ and Him crucified.

The cross is the power of God to those of us who believe. The cross takes us from being normal human beings and makes us what God wants us to be, extraordinary beings. We are not superior humans. We are a totally different species.

It is at the cross of Jesus that we identify our sin and are crucified with Christ. And, being crucified with Christ, we can experience new life in Him. The cross deals with the old person, the original man.

When we have died with Christ and been buried with Him in baptism, we can be raised in newness of life. At the cross, the old self, which is constantly struggling for supremacy, must give way.

Although we are born-again and have become children of God, we still live in these mortal bodies. Satan tries to use that fact to drag us down. He constantly reminds us that we live in a temporal world and are subject to temporal laws. In that way, he hopes to convince us that we are also subject to sin.

When we get sick, satan celebrates and uses the opportunity to claim that he has control over us. As our bodies age, he revels in the fact that we are still flesh and blood. He knows how to hurt us. He knows where our weaknesses lie. He knows where to tempt us.

Paul taught us what to do in these moments. We must reckon ourselves dead in Christ and alive unto God.

> *Likewise reckon ye also yourselves to be dead indeed unto sin, but alive unto God through Jesus Christ our Lord.*
>
> Romans 6:11, KJV

When satan comes to us and proposes his sin, we should say:

> *I'm sorry, but you have the wrong person. The person you are looking for died with Christ. I am a totally different person. I look like that old person and, for the sake of identification, I bear the same earthly name; but I am in no way the same person. He's dead.*

> *Jesus lives in me. He knows how to deal with temptation. He knows how to overcome. Nothing is too hard for Him. I reckon myself to be dead with Him and risen in new life.*

> *I have been crucified with Christ; and it is no longer I who live, but Christ lives in me; and the life which I now live in*

*the flesh I live by faith in the Son of God, who loved me, and
delivered Himself up for me.*

Galatians 2:20

The power of the cross is the power to be a new person.
It is the power to demonstrate the risen Lord Jesus in me. It
demonstrates that I can overcome temptation because He
overcomes temptation. It demonstrates that I can live because He lives.

When temptation comes our way, He puts Himself in
front of us to protect us. We overcome through Him. If you
try to overcome in the flesh, you will find that you are still
weak. But what you cannot do He can do. Let Him intervene
in your life. Let Him fight your battles. Let Him withstand
the blows the enemy has intended for your destruction.
Through the cross, you can conquer every foe. Through the
cross, you can deal with situations that have proven insur-
mountable to you until now. Give way to the power of the
Risen One.

No wonder Paul wanted to know nothing but Jesus Christ
and Him crucified! This is the power of God in action.

*Therefore from now on we recognize no man according to
the flesh; even though we have known Christ according to
the flesh, yet now we know Him thus no longer.*

2 Corinthians 5:16

We cannot think of Jesus now as He was in the flesh. He
is not hanging on a cross. He is no longer in the tomb. He is
risen. We do not picture in our minds the historical Christ
who walked the dusty roads of Nazareth as a humble car-
penter. Now we see Him as the risen and ascended Lord, as
the King of kings, as He who rules from Heaven.

In the same way, we must now look upon ourselves
differently. The cross made all the difference in our lives. We

are not carnal, earthy creatures any longer. We are more than conquerors through Christ. We can realize this truth only through the power of the cross.

The cross is not a popular message. There is nothing noble about it. It is a despicable emblem. We have tried to beautify it by making a cross of gold and wearing it as jewelry around our necks. But the fact remains. The cross of Jesus was ignoble. Crucifixion was a terrible way to die. If we had a choice, none of us would choose it as the method of preference.

Death itself is ugly and dishonorable. But crucifixion is the most agonizing, painful way to die. If that were not enough, those who were sentenced to crucifixion by the Romans were subjected first to public humiliation. They were stripped naked and hung publicly that way. Crowds gathered around and jeered at them in their dying moments. Blood flowed from many parts of the body, slowly weakening them. One by one, their bones were broken, increasing their agony. Yet this is the death that God ordained for His Son. The worst!

This is the message of the cross. Death! If we are to embrace the new life which Christ paid for on His cross, we must ourselves first die. Death brings life.

Truly, truly, I say to you, unless a grain of wheat falls into the earth and dies, it remains by itself alone; but if it dies, it bears much fruit.

John 12:24

It is not enough to be wounded with Christ; we must be crucified with Him.

How strange it is that modern day Christians are struggling to find every excuse to permit the flesh its life when only the death of the flesh brings complete life in Christ. Why do we struggle against that which brings victory?

While we are searching for excuses to spare the flesh, Jesus call goes forth:

> ..., "*If anyone wishes to come after Me, let him deny himself, and take up his cross, and follow Me.*"

> Matthew 16:24

Taking up the cross, to the first century believers, meant literally being willing to be crucified as Jesus was. Your cross may be less dramatic; but you must carry it nevertheless.

The Apostle Paul declared:

> ...*I die daily.*

> 1 Corinthians 15:31

Paul was a true follower of Christ. Every day he had to die to self. He had to be crucified, to enable Christ to live through him. The Christian life is not me being a better person, it is me getting out of the way so that Jesus can live His life through me. The Christian life is not me trying to find a way to obey the rules; it is me finding my way to the cross, so that His life can shine though me. It is me decreasing so that He can increase.

We decrease by way of the cross. He increases by way of the cross. We must exercise our faith to reckon ourselves dead with Him.

I have never said that this would be "fun." No one enjoys dying. The best way to handle this death is to get it over with quickly. Quickly submit to the will of God and let Him be Lord of your life. Too many people prolong the agony of this death. They try to do it in small stages. They die one nail at a time, one drop of blood at a time. No wonder they are miserable!

Reckon yourselves to be dead. Period! Get it over with and get on with new life in Christ. Let the power of the cross work in you today.

Chapter Twenty-four

The Power of the Spirit

But I say, walk by the Spirit, and you will not carry out the desire of the flesh. For the flesh sets its desire against the Spirit, and the Spirit against the flesh; for these are in opposition to one another, so that you may not do the things that you please. But if you are led by the Spirit, you are not under the Law. Now the deeds of the flesh are evident, which are: immorality, impurity, sensuality, idolatry, sorcery, enmities, strife, jealousy, outbursts of anger, disputes, dissensions, factions, envying, drunkenness, carousing, and things like these, of which I forewarn you just as I have forewarned you that those who practice such things shall not inherit the kingdom of God.

But the fruit of the Spirit is love, joy, peace, patience, kindness, goodness, faithfulness, gentleness, self-control; against such things there is no law. Now those who belong to Christ Jesus have crucified the flesh with its passions and desires. If we live by the Spirit, let us also walk by the Spirit.

Galatians 5:16-25

The power of the Spirit of God can bring us to victory over all the works of the flesh. The result of the working of God's Spirit in our lives, the *fruit* of the Spirit is: *love, joy, peace, patience, kindness, goodness, faithfulness, gentleness, and self-control*. That sounds like all the things we are striving for in life.

We often think of the power of the Spirit only as power to perform signs and wonders. We forget that it is power to live the Christian life victoriously.

When the Holy Spirit reigns in us, these fruit are resident in us. They become the natural way of living, the natural way of reacting to life's dilemmas. As we mature in the Spirit, the fruit of the Spirit matures in us, as well, perfecting our love and our peace, etc.

The fruit of the Spirit is the development of the character of Christ within us. It is this fruit, more than our words, that will attract other people to Christ. The Holy Spirit is God. His nature in us produces the nature of God Himself. He is loving, He is gentle. He is good. He is patient. He is kind. The power of the Spirit produces His life in us.

One of the purposes of Jesus' coming to the earth as man was to leave us an example. He said:

> ..."*Truly, truly, I say to you, the Son can do nothing of Himself, unless it is something He sees the Father doing; for whatever the Father does, these things the Son also does in like manner.*"

> John 5:19

The day that we stop living for self and allow God to demonstrate Himself in and through us, we will begin to demonstrate the same characteristics that were visible in the daily life of Jesus.

We often take on the characteristics or habits of people we are close to. They may be parents, mates or friends. Since that is true, we need to spend more time with Jesus. We need to stay in His presence—in prayer, worship and meditation on His Word—until His habits and characteristics begin to rub off on us.

If we are to be representatives of Christ, we should bear His nature to the world. Our failure to do this has given, at times, a mixed message to the lost. They like what we preach but not the way we live. We can overcome this problem by staying full of His Spirit. A life endued with the power of the Spirit will exude His nature. This was the very reason they called the early believers "Christians." Through the power of the Spirit, they had indeed become Christ-like and, because of that, were effective witnesses.

These three sources of power—the Word of God, the cross, and the Holy Spirit—work together to enable and equip us to do the work of the Lord. Don't go forth to battle without the power of all three in your life. The local church must return to the Source of her power if she is to go forth and fulfill her full destiny in God's eternal plan.

As an individual, know what sustains you, and you will never have reason to fail in your Christian experience.

Part V

My Challenge to YOU

Chapter Twenty-five

Kingdom Consciousness

And Jesus came up and spoke to them saying, "All authority has been given to Me in heaven and on earth. Go therefore and make disciples of all the nations, baptizing them in the name of the Father and the Son and the Holy Spirit, teaching them to observe all that I commanded you; and lo, I am with you always, even to the end of the age."

Matthew 28:18-20

The local church is made up of individuals. *"You are the body of Christ"* (1 Corinthians 12:27). It is impossible to speak about a strong local church without speaking of strong individuals. In closing, I want to challenge YOU.

It is not always easy to be faithful to our identity and to maintain our unique mission and message while still being relevant to the world in which we live. What are we to do? We are in this world, after all; and we are called to relate to the people around us so that we can win them to Christ. Yet we must remain loyal to our heavenly family. How can we achieve that difficult balance?

Some Christians adjust their mission in order to be understood by those around them. Others adjust their message so that it will no longer be totally alien to the people they live with from day to day. Most of us adjust our identity to some degree in order to "fit in" to our actual surroundings.

I am convinced that these acts of compromise are the reason so many believers are falling by the wayside today. I am convinced that, while there are many things we can to do relate to the people around us, these are three areas in which we simply cannot afford to compromise.

Our identity is unique:

We are not like other people. We are not interested in the same things. We don't think the same way or talk the same way. That means that we will be misunderstood by others. I say: SO BE IT! We cannot have it both ways. We cannot participate in the heavenly Kingdom and expect to be always understood and loved by those of this world's system. It is impossible. And why is this a problem? Are we ashamed to be Christians?

Personally, I am not ashamed to be an American. I would never hesitate to make my earthly citizenship known. In the same way, I am not ashamed to be a member of God's family, and I don't care who knows it. In fact, I am so proud of the fact that I am a new creature in Christ that I want everyone to know it. I have no problem with my ident.ty.

Our mission is unique:

The world tries to portray us as bigoted, narrow-minded, and self-centered. But we know that is not true. We have a mission in life, and nothing must be allowed to turn us aside from that mission. We do not think it unusual to be criticized and misunderstood. We accept that as part of the price we pay for excellence. We will not be deterred. We have a reason for living, and we will not compromise that mission, at whatever cost.

Our message is unique:

Although it can be adapted to people of various cultural settings, our message must never be altered in a way that it loses its necessary elements. When that happens, it is no longer the true Gospel. We simply cannot afford to make the Gospel "more palatable" to the lost. This is God's Word. Take it or leave it. I don't apologize for it. Ours is a wonderful message. Why change it?

The Kingdom of God is absolute. Jesus said, "*All authority has been given to Me.*" He did not say, "SOME authority has been given to ME." His total authority is the basis of our mission and our message. His Kingdom is absolute.

Everything is relevant to God's Kingdom, and God's Kingdom is relevant to everything. Nothing can happen in the world that is irrelevant to the Kingdom of God. The Kingdom of God is absolute!

Jesus rules over everything. If there were something over which He was not ruling, then He would not be the King of kings and the Lord of lords. If there were something over which He did not have jurisdiction, He could not be the Lord Jesus Christ. If there were some spot on the earth where He was not in control, or some person over which He had no rule, He could not be God.

That spot doesn't exist. That person has never been born. Jesus is Lord over all.

With this truth in mind, I challenge YOU today to consider anew your proper identity or **posture**. Do you really want to be part of this sin-cursed world? Wouldn't you rather be part of God's eternal Kingdom?

With this truth in mind, I challenge YOU today to consider anew your mission or **purpose** in life. Do you really want to live your entire lifetime just for the accumulation of "things"? Wouldn't you much rather accomplish a divine purpose in life, carry out the vision of the heart of God and know that your life has counted for eternity?

With this truth in mind, I challenge YOU today to consider anew your message or **proclamation**. Do you really want to continue to parrot the party line, repeating the empty cliches you hear on television talk shows or insisting on the opinions of today's "experts"? Wouldn't you rather be a part of spreading the eternal and incorruptible Word of an unfailing God?

With this truth in mind, I challenge YOU today to consider anew the Source of your **power**. In your own strength you cannot overcome the enemies arrayed against you, but with God's power on your side, you "overwhelmingly conquer." Don't abandon your Source of power, even for a moment.

God has a great plan for YOUR life. YOU are His child. He has designed special gifts for YOUR use. He has promised to empower YOU with His Spirit to make them work. He has given YOU a place in His glorious harvest of souls and given YOU the privilege of reaching out with YOUR sickle to the ends of the earth to reap in these last days.